JAZZIN' ABOUT
fun pieces for
PIANO/KEYBOARD

CONTENTS

PAM WEDGWOOD

FABER *ff* MUSIC

TO THE TEACHER

Jazzin' About is an original collection of pieces in a variety of rock and jazz styles.

It is arranged broadly in order of increasing difficulty and I hope that you will find it a useful addition to any teaching programme, providing a firm foundation for more advanced study of this style of playing. If the student plays an electronic keyboard the use of suitable drum beats will help to achieve rhythmic accuracy – a fundamental necessity for good rock and jazz-style playing.

One of the most important aspects of teaching a musical instrument is to ensure that the student enjoys what he or she plays. The study of varied idioms will encourage the pupil to progress faster both technically and musically.

TO THE STUDENT

My primary reason for writing **Jazzin' About** is to give you an opportunity to play in popular styles while you are in the earlier stages of your musical development. Jazz, Rock and Blues are all part of our musical heritage and should be experienced along with more 'classically' orientated works. However, learning to master popular rhythms can be hard work as well as fun! Once you have learnt each piece, try to put a little of your own expression and style into it – and then see if you can improvise some of your own!

I hope that **Jazzin' About** will give you new enthusiasm for your keyboard playing.

Pamela Wedgwood

© 1989 by Faber Music Ltd
First published in 1989 by Faber Music Ltd
3 Queen Square London WC1N 3AU
Cover by velladesign
Music engraved by Sambo Music Engraving Co
Printed in England by Caligraving Ltd

ISBN 0-571-51105-8

To buy Faber Music publications or to find out about the full range of titles available please contact your local music retailer or Faber Music sales enquiries:

Faber Music Limited, Burnt Mill, Elizabeth Way, Harlow, CM20 2HX England
Tel: +44 (0)1279 82 89 82   Fax: +44 (0)1279 82 89 83
sales@fabermusic.com   www.fabermusic.com

1. Take it from here

2.   Summer Song

3. Why?

Quite slow and gentle ♩ = 96

4. The Stranger

5.   Pink Lady

6. Never let go

7.   Just passing by

8. Jack in a Juke Box

9. Laid-back Blues

10.   Back to the Wall

11.   Wheels of Time

Printed by
Halstan & Co. Ltd., Amersham, Bucks., England

The JAZZIN' ABOUT Series

PAM WEDGWOOD

Christmas Jazzin' About. Piano   ISBN 0-571-51507-X

Christmas Jazzin' About. Piano Duet   ISBN 0-571-51584-3

Christmas Jazzin' About. Violin   ISBN 0-571-51694-7

Christmas Jazzin' About. Cello   ISBN 0-571-51695-5

Christmas Jazzin' About. Flute   ISBN 0-571-51586-X

Christmas Jazzin' About. Clarinet   ISBN 0-571-51585-1

Christmas Jazzin' About. Alto Saxophone   ISBN 0-571-51587-8

Christmas Jazzin' About. Trumpet   ISBN 0-571-51696-3

Easy Jazzin' About. Piano   ISBN 0-571-51337-9

Easy Jazzin' About. Piano Duets   ISBN 0-571-51661-0

Green Jazzin' About. Piano   ISBN 0-571-51645-9

Jazzin' About. Piano   ISBN 0-571-51105-8

Jazzin' About. Piano Duets   ISBN 0-571-51662-9

Jazzin' About. Violin   ISBN 0-571-51315-8

Jazzin' About. Cello   ISBN 0-571-51316-6

Jazzin' About. Flute   ISBN 0-571-51275-5

Jazzin' About. Clarinet   ISBN 0-571-51273-9

Jazzin' About. Alto Saxophone   ISBN 0-571-51054-X

Jazzin' About. Trumpet   ISBN 0-571-51039-6

Jazzin' About. Trombone   ISBN 0-571-51053-1

Jazzin' About Styles. Piano   ISBN 0-571-51718-8

More Jazzin' About. Piano   ISBN 0-571-51437-5

Really Easy Jazzin' About. Piano   ISBN 0-571-52089-8

FABER _ff_ MUSIC